Coming Soon...

BABOONS WAITED ON TABLES IN ANCIENT EGYPT
WEIRD FACTS ABOUT CIVILIZATIONS

FLIES TASTE WITH THEIR FEET
WEIRD FACTS ABOUT INSECTS

FROGS SWALLOW WITH THEIR EYES!

WEIRD FACTS ABOUT
FROGS, SNAKES, TURTLES, & LIZARDS

A WEIRD-BUT-TRUE BOOK

by
Melvin & Gilda Berger
illustrated by Robert Roper

SCHOLASTIC INC.
New York Toronto London Auckland Sydney

ISBN 0-590-93778-2

Text copyright © 1996 by The Gilda Berger Revocable Trust.
Illustrations copyright © 1996 by Bob Roper
All rights reserved. Published by Scholastic Inc.

12 11 10 9 8 7 6 5   8 9/9 0 1/0

Printed in the U.S.A.   40

First Scholastic printing, September 1996

FROGS

FROGS SWALLOW WITH THEIR EYES

Frogs swallow in the wackiest way. A frog catches bugs in its mouth. Then it blinks. This presses the eyeballs down against the roof of the mouth. The roof bends and pushes the bugs into the frog's stomach! All in the blink of an eye!

DID YOU KNOW?

- **Frogs' tongues have lots of taste buds.**
- **They spit out food that tastes bad.**

GROSS GRUB

Most frogs eat a steady diet of insects, worms, and spiders. But sometimes a frog has a real treat. It swallows its skin!

A frog sheds its skin a few times a year. With its front legs, it pulls the old skin off over its head — and pops it into its mouth!

FROG OR SPONGE?

No one has ever seen frogs drink water. It's not that they don't get thirsty. They just soak up all the water they need through their skin!

LAUGH LINES

The frog jumped into the soda because he thought it was Croaka-Cola!

GOGGLE EYES

Frogs' eyes stick out from their heads. Each eye looks like a tiny periscope on a submarine. Popping eyes let frogs see in all directions — front, sides, *and* back. They make catching bugs a snap!

Eyes that stick out also help frogs hide in ponds or lakes. They can stay underwater while keeping their eyes out for trouble — or their next meal. Try sneaking up on a frog and you'll see what we mean!

NEVER KISS A FROG

In a fairy tale, a princess kisses a frog and the frog turns into a handsome prince. But not in real life! Many kinds of frogs are poisonous. Their skins taste awful. Even a little peck could be horrible!

NUMBER-ONE KILLER

People in South America keep away from the **golden poison dart frog**. Each of these little creatures has enough poison to kill 1,500 people!

LAUGH LINES

How can you avoid being killed by biting poison frogs?

Don't bite any!

DEADLY ARROWS

Hunters in tropical rain forests kill different kinds of poison frogs and dip their arrows into the poison. They shoot big animals, such as jaguars, with the arrows. Animals hit with poisoned arrows die in minutes!

FROG TALK

Frogs have vocal cords in their throats, just as we do. They force air past the cords to make all kinds of froggy sounds.

- The **barking frog** sounds like — you guessed it — a barking dog.

- The **wood frog** quacks like a duck.

- **Eastern narrow-mouthed toads** bleat like lambs.

- The **Mexican tree frog** makes a noise like a car engine starting.

- **Carpenter frogs** sound like someone is hammering nails.

- The **northern cricket frog** calls "Gick, gick, gick" once a second.

FOR THE RECORD

Biggest: The **goliath frog** of Africa. A record-breaker caught in 1989 weighed just over eight pounds! With its legs outstretched, the frog was the size of a three-year-old child!

Smallest: The **Cuban arrow-poison frog**. Fully grown, it is only about a half-inch long. Its whole body can fit on your thumbnail!

SURPRISE EGGS

You may think that frog eggs hatch into frogs. They don't. Frog eggs hatch into fishlike tadpoles. It takes a few months for tadpoles to change into frogs.

BIG FAMILIES

Female **bullfrogs** lay up to 20,000 eggs at a time. If all the eggs hatched, ponds and lakes would be thick with tadpoles and bullfrogs. Actually, only a few eggs make it. Most are eaten by birds, snakes, and other animals.

?

- **The bullfrog is the largest frog native to the United States**

THE BACKWARDS FROG

Most frogs start as tiny eggs, become little tadpoles, and grow into full-sized frogs. But the **paradoxical frog** grows in the opposite way. It shrinks from an eight-inch tadpole down to a two-inch frog!

PECULIAR POPS

After the female **Darwin frog** hatches her eggs, the male does something weird. He *swallows* the tadpoles! He holds up to twenty tadpoles in his throat. As soon as the tadpoles change into little frogs, the male spits them out.

The female **midwife toad** lays her eggs in two long strings. The male then winds the strings around his rear legs! For about three weeks, he drags the eggs around. Finally he drops them into the water. And presto — the eggs turn into tadpoles!

SUPER MOMS

The female **Suriname toad** keeps her eggs in an odd place — on her back! The eggs are fertilized when the female toad is upside down. As she turns over onto her back, she rubs the eggs into her skin. Because the eggs are gummy, they stick there. A few months later, the eggs hatch — and the tiny toads are on their own!

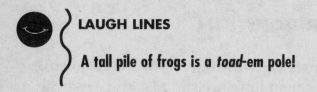

LAUGH LINES

A tall pile of frogs is a *toad*-em pole!

A BUM RAP

Toads are fatter and darker than frogs. They also have bumps on their skin that look like warts. Does that mean that touching toads gives you warts? Not at all! Warts come from viruses. Touching a toad will *never* make your skin bumpy!

DID YOU KNOW?

- When it gets very hot, toads dig deep into the ground and live there.

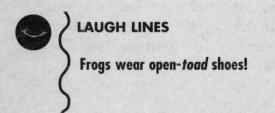

LAUGH LINES

Frogs wear open-*toad* shoes!

SEE-THROUGH SKIN

The **glass frog** of Central America hides nothing. You can look right through its skin and see its heart, lungs, and other organs. A close look even shows the tree branch on which the frog is sitting!

SPRING FASHION

The well-dressed male **hairy frog** of Africa wears a pale, tan "skirt" in the springtime! The skirt is really thin blood vessels that hang outside the frog's body. The high style catches the eye of female hairy frogs!

JUMPING JOCKS

Every year is "leap" year for frogs. Long, strong back legs make frogs amazing jumpers. In 1977 a **South African sharp-nosed frog** covered 33 feet in a triple leap! That's the length of two cars.

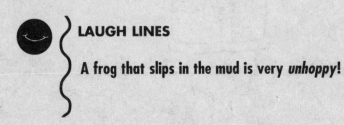

LAUGH LINES

A frog that slips in the mud is very *unhoppy!*

IT'S RAINING FROGS!

Tornadoes or powerful winds sometimes sweep frogs up from lakes, rivers, and ponds. The gusts blow the frogs into the air and then drop them down. On such days, it's good to carry an umbrella!

DID YOU KNOW?

- **Frogs rained down on Trowbridge, England, in 1939 and on Memphis, Tennessee, in 1946.**

SNAKES

PIGGY SNAKES

Snakes have the most disgusting table manners. When a snake eats, it opens its mouth very, very wide. Often it stuffs in a whole, live animal — anything from a rat or rabbit to an entire pig or goat! Even worse, the snake swallows its food without chewing! You can sometimes see the bulge as the animal passes through the snake's body.

DID YOU KNOW?

- **Most snakes don't need to eat very often.**
- **One big meal can last for many months.**

LAUGH LINES

What do you call a rabbit who comes near a snake?

Dinner!

A TONGUE FOR A NOSE

A snake flicks out its tongue as it slides along the ground. It's the snake's way of smelling. The tongue brings the odors to the roof of the snake's mouth. Maybe the snake smells a rat — or maybe it just smells trouble!

LAUGH LINES

CAMPER: I thought you said this camp has no snakes.

COUNSELOR: That's right. These snakes come from the camp down the road.

"HEARING" WITHOUT EARS

Bang a drum and the snake hears nothing. But tiptoe nearby — and the snake immediately knows you're there! Snakes have no ears. But they pick up vibrations from the ground with their skull bones. Now that's really using your head!

WIDE-EYED WONDERS

Snakes don't have eyelids! Their eyes are always open. Instead of eyelids, their eyes are covered by a clear scale. It's impossible to tell whether a snake is asleep or awake — until it's too late!

"FANGS" A LOT

Poisonous snakes bite with long, hollow teeth, called fangs. The fangs are like giant hypodermic needles that squirt out poison. It takes just one bite to kill.

DID YOU KNOW?

- Snakes use their teeth for biting and holding, not for chewing.

LAUGH LINES

Will a snake bite you if you're carrying a flashlight?

It depends on how fast you're running with it!

READY, AIM, SPIT

When scared, the **spitting cobra** of Africa rises up and squirts poison — right into the enemy's eyes! The stream of venom can reach about eight feet. A direct hit blinds.

DID YOU KNOW?

- The spitting cobra squeezes poison out through holes at the tips of its fangs. It can squirt six times before its supply runs out. A day or so later, it's back in business.

WARNING RATTLES

The **rattlesnake** has a built-in alarm in its tail. When it shakes its tail, several hard rings, or rattles, bump against one another. The noise can be heard up to 100 feet away. It's enough to make most animals run away — fast!

DID YOU KNOW?

- The rattles on a snake's tail are made of the same material as your fingernails.

LAUGH LINES

BOB: I just saw a baby snake.

ROB: How did you know it was a baby?

BOB: It was shaking a rattle!

FOR THE RECORD

Biggest: The **anaconda** of South America can grow up to 29 feet 11 inches long and weigh an amazing 500 pounds!

Smallest: If you took the lead out of a pencil, the tiny **thread snake** could fit in the hole!

Longest: The **python** measures nearly 33 feet! In a zoo, it takes twelve strong keepers to carry one adult python.

Fastest: The **black mamba snake** has been clocked in short bursts at speeds as high as 7 miles an hour.

LAUGH LINES

Why do they measure snakes in inches?

Because snakes have no feet!

SNAKE CHARMING

The snake charmer plays a flutelike instrument. It looks as if the snake is dancing to the music. But the snake moves only because the man is rocking from

side to side. It is on guard and ready to charge —
and bite. And that would not be at all charming!

DID YOU KNOW?

- Snakes probably developed from lizards about 100
  million years ago. These ancient creatures burrowed
  underground and had little use for their legs.

LAUGH LINES

SNAKE CHARMER: **What would you do if a snake charged
you?**

KID: **I'd pay whatever it charged!**

HAVING A BALL

The **African ball python** protects itself in a special
way. It tucks in its head and coils up into a tight ball!
The python stays that way until it is safe to come
out. You can roll the ball-shaped snake along the
ground. But don't try to bounce it!

PUTTING ON A SHOW

The **hognose snake** has a full bag of tricks. When an enemy comes near, the hognose raises its head and shakes its tail — just like a rattlesnake. It also hisses loudly and puffs out its neck to look bigger. Finally it springs forward. Alas, its bite is harmless!

If that doesn't work, the hognose snake pulls another stunt. It turns over onto its back, opens its mouth with its tongue hanging out, and plays dead. The inside of its mouth looks like rotting meat — and the snake smells just as bad! Most animals leave — they probably lose their appetites.

A TWO-HEADED FAKE

It's sometimes hard to tell whether the **rubber boa** is coming or going. That's because it has a real head at one end and a fake head at the other end!

When in danger, the rubber boa coils up into a tight ball. It tucks its real head safely underneath, and it sticks its fake head up into the air. Most enemies attack the fake head. We can guess that the rubber boa prefers a bite on its tail to a bite on its head!

SNAKE OR FROG?

Everyone knows that snakes slide along the ground and frogs jump into the air. Everyone, that is, except the **jumping viper** of Central America. If it sees a bird on a low tree limb, the jumping viper forms its body into a round coil on the ground. Then it springs two feet straight up in the air and grabs the unlucky bird!

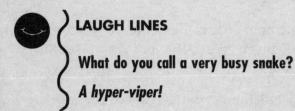

GIANT KILLER

Elephants fear no animal — except the **king cobra**. This snake attacks an elephant at two places: the tender tip of its trunk and the points where the elephant's toenails meet its foot. A snakebite at either place can topple a huge elephant!

DID YOU KNOW?

- King cobras strike and kill about 10,000 people a year in India. Most die within an hour of being bitten. In fact, just one ounce of poison from a king cobra could kill more than 4,000 people!

LOOK-ALIKES

The **coral snake** and the **milk snake** are look-alikes. They are both red with black and yellow bands. But the coral snake is poisonous and dangerous. The milk snake is harmless.

Being a look-alike helps the milk snake. Any animal that survives a run-in with the poisonous coral snake will stay away from the look-alike milk snake.

Here's a way to tell them apart. The coral snake's three bands are yellow, black, yellow. The milk

snake's bands are reversed — black, yellow, black. This rhyme will help you remember which is which:

> Red next to black,
> Friend of Jack.
> Red next to yellow,
> Can kill a fellow.

DID YOU KNOW?

- **The country of Myanmar leads the world in snakebites. For every 100,000 people, about 15 ½ get bitten each year. (The half persons are probably bitten by very small snakes!)**

LAUGH LINES

What steps should you take if you see a coral snake?

Very big ones!

UNDERGROUND SNAKES

Blind snakes dig tunnels in the soil. They eat the ants, worms, and termites that crawl through the earth. These snakes can hardly see. After all, what good is sight for hunting underground?

A RAFT OF TROUBLE

In 1932 sailors sighted a giant 10-foot-wide and 70-foot-long raft in the Indian Ocean. But this raft wasn't made of wood. And no one would dare sail on it. The raft was formed of many thousands of poisonous **sea snakes**! The tide had probably pushed them all together.

? | **DID YOU KNOW?**

- Sea snakes are among the most poisonous snakes of all. A bite can kill a human in just over two hours.

TURTLES

TOOTHLESS WONDERS

It's true. Turtles don't have any teeth. Yet the edges of their beaks are very sharp. They can slice through most plants and animals. Their powerful jaws can even bite through wood!

LAUGH LINES

Turtles have short tempers. They are always snapping!

SUITS OF ARMOR

When frightened, most turtles scrunch their heads, legs, and tails into their shells. Many even clamp the top and bottom parts of their shells together. Once inside, turtles are as safe as knights in armor.

DID YOU KNOW?

- The shell is part of the turtle's skeleton. The turtle is the only large animal with part of its skeleton on the *outside*!

LONG LIVE THE TURTLES

Turtles live longer than any other animal. In 1766 someone brought a full-grown turtle to an island in the Indian Ocean. The turtle lived there for 152 years. Then in 1918 it fell off a wall and was killed. Experts guess that the turtle was about 170 years old when it died! No one knows how long it would have lived had it not fallen.

DID YOU KNOW?

- Turtles were here long before the dinosaurs. By now, the dinosaurs have been gone for 65 million years. But turtles are still around.

THE QUIET LIFE

Do you like to sleep late in the morning and hang around all day? Then you would love the life of a tortoise. Many tortoises sleep up to 16 hours a day. They spend most of the rest of the time basking in the sun. Maybe that's why they live so long!

LIFE IN THE SLOW LANE

A tortoise is a turtle that lives on land. In *The Tortoise and the Hare*, the tortoise wins the race. But in real life, you could easily beat a tortoise. In a one-mile race, you would cross the finish line in about ten or fifteen minutes. If it didn't stop to eat, the tortoise would reach the end five hours later!

LIFE IN THE FAST LANE

The **leatherback sea turtle** can swim a mile in less than three minutes! A champion human swimmer takes five minutes to swim the same distance. But don't forget, sea turtles can't do the backstroke!

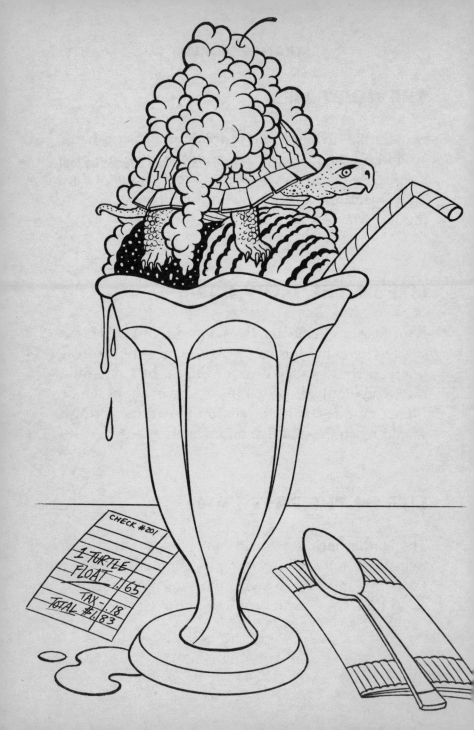

How do you make a turtle float?

Two scoops of ice cream, soda water, and a turtle on top!

FOR THE RECORD

Biggest: A huge **leatherback turtle** washed up on a beach in Wales in 1988. It was 9 $\frac{1}{2}$ feet long — the size of a large sofa. It weighed 2,120 pounds, which is more than a ton!

Smallest: The **eastern mud turtle** is only three or four inches long. It can fit in the palm of your hand!

MYSTERY UPON MYSTERY

Once every three years, the female **green turtles** of South America do something really bizarre. They swim 1,200 miles from the coast of Brazil to Ascension Island in the middle of the Atlantic Ocean! The turtles lay their eggs on the same beach where they were born. Then they cover their eggs with sand, drag themselves back into the water, and swim home.

About two months later, the eggs hatch. But the newborn turtles never see their moms or dads. They are on their own right from the start!

Here are the mysteries:

- Where do the turtles get the strength to swim 1,200 miles each way?

- What guides them to the tiny island, which is less than seven miles long and five miles wide?

- How do they find the right beach?

- Why do they swim so far to lay their eggs?

DID YOU KNOW?

- The green turtle is nearly extinct because so many people use it to make soup.

LAUGH LINES

Why do green turtles swim across the ocean?

To get to the other tide!

GOING FISHING

Two kinds of turtles "fish" with their own built-in bait. The **alligator snapping turtle** dangles its tongue in the water. Sticking up from the tongue is a pink flap that looks like a small, wiggly worm. When a fish goes for the flap, the turtle snaps its jaws down on the prey. So long, fish!

The **matamata turtle** fishes with the short, thin lengths of skin that hang from its neck. The turtle stands in a muddy river and the weedlike threads drift in the water. When an unlucky fish swims toward the skin-bait, the turtle nabs it.

DID YOU KNOW?

- **The shell of the alligator snapping turtle is the same color as the muddy river waters where it lives.**

HORRIBLY SMELLY

Can you imagine naming an animal "stinkpot"? Yet it's the perfect name for this turtle. When attacked, the **stinkpot turtle** gives off a disgusting smell. One whiff is all it takes. The enemy flees — and the turtle is safe.

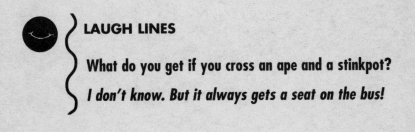

LAUGH LINES

What do you get if you cross an ape and a stinkpot?

I don't know. But it always gets a seat on the bus!

TORTOISE PETS

The people of Madagascar love and respect the **radiated tortoise**. Often, they keep these turtles as pets. They believe the radiated tortoise has many special powers. They keep these animals as pets and will not harm them in any way.

LAUGH LINES

The owner of a tortoise goes to a pet store.
"I want to buy my pet tortoise a sweater," she says.
"Bring in the tortoise so we can find the right size," the clerk replies.
"Oh, no," says the woman. "I want this to be a surprise!"

LIZARDS

BITES THAT KILL

Never mess with the 16-inch-long **Gila monster**! When it bites, poison flows into the wound. Less than an ounce of its venom can kill an adult human! It takes much less than that to kill the small animals the Gila monster usually eats. Still, the Gila monster is not greedy. After a big meal it may not eat again for over a year!

DID YOU KNOW?

- There are thirty-four known cases of Gila monster attacks on humans. Eight of those people died from their wounds. The rest lived to tell the story.

LAUGH LINES

MIKE: That's a friendly Gila monster. It'll eat off your hand.

IKE: That's what I'm afraid of!

FOR THE RECORD

Biggest: The **Komodo dragon** is the largest lizard. One in the St. Louis Zoo was over ten feet long and tipped the scale at 365 pounds!

Smallest: The **least gecko** is only about a half inch long and weighs only a few ounces. Yet you can hear this noisy little beast six miles away!

Fastest: In 1941, a **six-lined racerunner** was clocked speeding along at an amazing 18 miles an hour!

TEMPER, TEMPER

The **horned toad lizard** is named for its toadlike body. When it gets angry you'd better watch out. It shoots bright red blood out of its eyes! The blood that streams from the horned toad can travel more than a yard. It won't do you any harm, but the sight could scare you half to death!

?

DID YOU KNOW?

- Farmers like the horned toad lizard because it eats insects that destroy food crops. Texas Christian University made the horned toad lizard its mascot.

A REAL-LIFE DRAGON

Dragons in storybooks have wings and claws and breathe fire. The real-life Komodo dragon is a huge lizard. It eats pigs, goats, deer — and even humans. Luckily the Komodo dragon lives only on Komodo and a few other islands in Indonesia.

The fierce Komodo dragon usually bites a victim's leg to stop its escape. The dragon then quickly rips the prey apart and eats the flesh. The germs in a Komodo dragon's mouth will kill its prey within two days.

A Komodo dragon once ate a whole one hundred-pound pig in 15 minutes! Sometimes it will eat more than its own weight at one time. Can you imagine overeating like that?

WALK ON WATER

The silly-looking **basilisk** lives in tropical rain forests. And it walks on water! When fleeing an enemy, the basilisk darts across a pond or stream on its two back feet. It is so fast and light that it stays on top. Don't try this trick yourself — unless, of course, you're some sort of water bug!

THE AMAZING GECKO

The **gecko** is a champion gymnast. It can walk up walls and cross ceilings *upside down*! Its toes have pads with thousands of short, stiff bristles that grab surfaces. Grabby toes let the gecko walk almost anywhere!

And the gecko has a wild way to clean its eyes. It flicks out its long tongue and licks the dirt away! Maybe that's why you never see a gecko wearing goggles.

LAUGH LINES

The lizard who wants to learn about money studies *gecko*-nomics!

A CREATURE'S FEATURES

Most lizards have two eyes. But not the **tuatara**. It has a "third eye" in the middle of its head! What a job it would be to fit a tuatara with eyeglasses!

When active, the tuatara breathes about eight times a minute. You and I breathe more than twice as fast. But at rest, the tuatara takes only *one breath an hour*! This is astounding. We can't even go two minutes without breathing.

GROWING A NEW TAIL

Birds and snakes often bite the bright blue tail of the **blue-tailed skink**. What happens next is spooky. The tail snaps right off! Then it wiggles around on the ground! While the attacker watches the tail, the lizard escapes — leaving its tail behind.

Believe it or not, the skink does not miss its tail. It soon grows another! The new tail is usually a little shorter and plumper than the old one — and just as good at saving the skink's life.

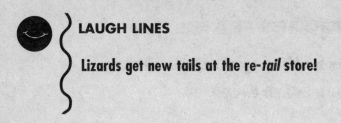

LAUGH LINES

Lizards get new tails at the re-*tail* store!

TONGUE TIED

Everyone knows it's rude to stick out your tongue. But the Australian **blue-tongued skink** sticks out its tongue to save its life! When threatened, the skink opens its mouth wide and waves its long, bright blue tongue. The tongue looks so horrid that most attackers forget to strike.

DID YOU KNOW?

- Many kinds of lizards that lose their tails can grow new ones.

BEST BLUFFER

If an enemy comes near, the frightened Australian **frilled lizard** tries to flee. If it can't get away, it bluffs its enemy. The lizard spins around, rears up on its back legs, and opens its mouth wide. At the same time, it spreads out a huge collar around its head! This makes it look many times bigger and fiercer than it really is.

If the bluff fails, the frilled lizard runs forward, swaying from side to side. It whips its long tail back and forth and hisses loudly. This usually scares away even the biggest bully!

QUICK-CHANGE ARTISTS

Chameleons can change colors — yellow, green, white, red, brown, or black! Most people believe they change colors to match their backgrounds. But

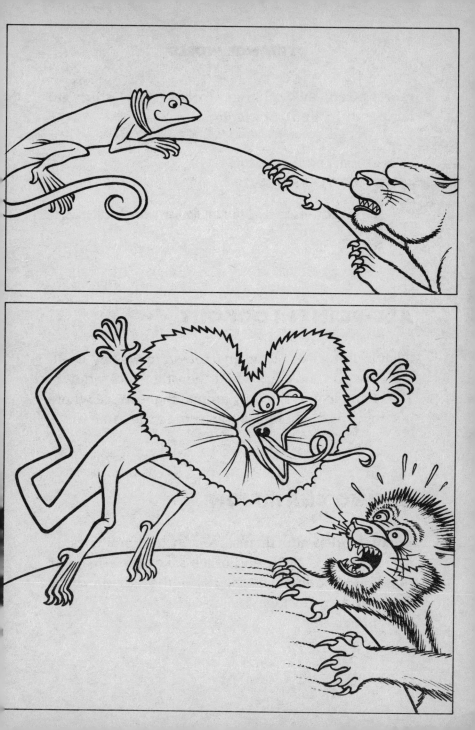

more often they change to adapt to shifts in temperature, light, or emotion.

? | **DID YOU KNOW?**

• **Chameleons tend to turn darker when frightened.**

ALL-POINTS LOOKOUT

Each bulging eye of the chameleon moves by itself. One eye can look up while the other looks down. The chameleon is the only animal that can see where it's going and where it came from at the same time!

DIVING CHAMPION

Iguanas often sun themselves on tree branches. A favorite spot is at the end of a limb over a stream or pond. If in danger — *swoosh* — the iguana dives down and swims away!

A HOLE IN THE HEAD

The sea-dwelling **marine iguana** gets rid of extra salt in its body in a gross way. It blows the salt out through a hole in its snout! As far as anyone knows, that's the only reason for the hole.

LAUGH LINES

What did the iguana say when it met the monster?

"Iguana go home!"

A MIXED-UP ANIMAL

Whoever named the **blindworm** got it all wrong. The blindworm is not blind nor is it a worm. It's a lizard — that looks like a snake!

CRACKED UP

When in trouble, the **chuckwalla lizard** heads for the nearest crack in a rock. The lizard slides inside and puffs up its body. It fits so snugly that no animal can pull it out!

DANCING LIZARDS

The **fringe-toed lizards** of Africa often seem to be dancing. They jump around, kicking up one foot after another. Sometimes they raise all four feet and flop down on their stomachs! What are they doing? Just trying to cool off their feet from the hot desert sand.

LAUGH LINES

A woman was walking with a big lizard.
A police officer saw her and said, "Take that lizard to the zoo."
The next day the police officer again saw the woman with the lizard. "I thought I told you to take that lizard to the zoo," the officer said.
"I did," the woman answered. "Today I'm taking it to the movies!"